Am I or the others crazy?

Fay Youance

Presentation by *BookLeaf Publishing*

Web: www.bookleafpub.com

E-mail: info@bookleafpub.com

ISBN: 9789357615464

First edition 2022

This book is for everyone struggling with BPD, often let down by professionals and their support system as well as any other human for whom life feels a little too hard to keep going most of the time. Bravo! You're still here with us.

The lottery

I never was great at arithmetic.
When I found myself entranced by the numbers
I could never stop counting my failures.

Counting;
Every second.
Counting;
Every minute.
Counting;
Every hour.

Counting.

The days till I feel okay.
The weeks till I truly feel fulfilled.
The years till I finally feel at piece.

Counting;
Family members that have abandoned me or
were never there.
Counting;
Fake friends I glorified because I can never
stand being alone
Counting;

The lies thrown at me like I can't see past their
mirage.

I've learned I cannot build a life for myself
without losing a piece or two. Or three. Or four.
So I am always here... counting.

Apparently, every moment has value.
So until there's nothing else to;
I'll keep counting to the next life.

Two to five

He stepped into that box willingly,
considering his last chance to flee.

One last longing look
to their abandoned prodigy.

Borderline living

Battered brain
Bruised body

Burned memories
Borderline realities

Hopeless letter to the gods

Today I feel alive, yet apprehensive about the
future
knowing it never lasts.

I dread feeling by fear I'll feel
too much too fast, too deeply.

The Gods laugh at my pain,
Mistake impatience for weakness.

Maybe I am weak.
Maybe I deserve the pain.
Maybe this is retribution.

For what?

Clueless to the wrongs my past has committed,
For which I am now paying their price;
In cold blood and torn flesh;
In enough tears to drown my deepest sorrows;

Enough hurt to drown the haunting voices
Making restful sleep unachievable.
Rest my soul, I need it.

I need it. I need it PLEASE!
I beg of you, let me rest.

Let me rest.
Let me die.

So I may live again
I want to live again.

And live?
And live.

So you shall find me again.
And again and again.

unReal

7

When it comes for me
Friend, Foe, I will not resist
My mind, my escape.

Visit to the sandbox

There once was a little girl,
skin of honey, head of stone

She dreamed of Yellow in that grey box
Replaced smiles on their square faces

She wished Big Head happy thoughts
Longed for uninterrupted embraces

She witnessed the Matron's faith fray,
Crumbled as the scary man took Yellow away.

Beliefs

They flow as water.
Do be careful not to drown
in the fantasy

Hungry beasts

Replaced by diaphanous impostors
Few find their way to their posts
Few dare slip past my guards
Knowing they'll be found and expelled at last

They shouldn't have made their way in,
Yet stray to see me suffer for my lack of
discipline
And I gaze from afar like a predator
Until I give in, remembering the terror

Years past, we're strangers with a subtle sense of
familiarity
Our reunion tainted by lingering insecurity
Empty and drained in that place that should be
full
That place that should be safe, void

Alien touch

At night I wonder,
When our lips become strangers
Will you still love me?

Tipping point

as i lay here barely breathing
as tightly rolled as i can
hugging myself for some
semblance of comfort
burning. freezing water
showering my body
my sleepwear slick with snot
sticking to my silhouette

Where can I escape?

my screams bouncing off the walls
hitting back where they came from
my sobs drowned by the rain that should
alleviate my pain
my jumbled thoughts fighting themselves to gain
control
my bile rising again like my rotten corpse in the
lake
when The Storm, seems to slow, it tricks me and
hurts me à nouveau

Where can I escape?

when the storms surrounding the gates are so
powerful
both with the power to destroy one another
both willing to yield it to prove themselves right
both focused on foolish feelings instead of the
elephant in the room
just laying there, its blood muddled
with the growing puddle at their feet

Where can I escape?

when i'm trapped in a room w a dead reflection
of what i used to be
can i break the mirrors or once more
will i use them to bleed
as the animal looks into my cold dead eyes,
I know,
finally

There is no escape from reality.

The dive

My orphan soul weeping in melancholy
I peek, aching for the strength to call
reinforcements
Spellbound by these seductive shadows
I take the plunge, trusting it to heal all ailments.

Lover

Why don't you love me
Who could ever replace us
Was it always fake?

Reflections

I try to build myself up,
But she needs pain.
She needs blood.

She wants my dreams, my hope, my future
She wants my trust, my love, my life
She wants my joy, my peace of mind

But she's a piece of my mind
And I can't destroy her because
She is me and I am She.

So, I destroy her
Because I am me and I am weak
And she's stronger

So I feed her my pain and my cries again.
And again. And again.

To destroy us.

Thievery

I trusted them with intimate knowledge.

They once were my safety, my shelter, my haven
In a different light, I saw them unbothered,
relentless, ruthless,
They robbed my body blind and left me barren

Enlightened, I know my safety was simulated
nonetheless

I trusted them… and they buried me.

Monsters

It begins once we're hyperaware
A few subtle changes here and there
Atoms feel heavier, oxygen seems to run low
As if buried in quicksand, you sink, oh so slow

Cold sweat trickling down, warm skin in
contrast
They smother you, get your heart beating fast
Inch by inch, your body fills with anticipation
Preparing for the worst, even your imagination

Burning tears form, your vision blurring,
Anxiety in your throat has your words slurring
Room spinning, walls closing, you're alone
Your archenemy's location unknown

Afraid and unnerved, you go hunting
In your ears a deafening ringing
Your unimpressive weapon and teeth clenched
You delude yourself with bravery, your terror
entrenched

Shaking, you find yourself raising your
instrument

Unprompted, your feet creep upon the
horrendous beast
You freeze, frightful in the face of your assailant
Finally, surrendering to the fear, your mind is
released

Scarlet

I've grown to be terrified of the twilight
Awake, nightmares swirling behind my open
eyes
Unsettled, I see demons all around, bracing for a
fight

I focus on the red halos that protect me,
The crimson glow brought back my sanity
Camouflaged by the blood, demons can't find
me

COD: Greed

What happened to home?

People used to care about community and the
planet.
Living a fulfilling life, feeling at peace used to
be the dream
How to remain optimistic about the future with
the present so bleak?

Older transgressors look down on us when
speaking our truth
And call us weak for remaining strong, always
blaming youth
They take no accountability for the disaster we
inherited

Care, concern and compassion are now rare
currency
So blinded by self-interest, living in disharmony
Why aren't they screaming, howling, begging
for change?

We see corruption at the highest levels
thriving, festering through the fissures
of a system meant to keep us obedient

Some people scared to go outside to get blown
up,
Others can't get inside, too busy trying to catch
up
Neither has a home

We see children, skin taut over their bones
begging to survive
Across the water, others, ungrateful for the
excess in their lives
Neither is happy, but one is superior

Corpses of creatures who'll disappear in our
lifetime
The purest element polluted, tainted by
overconsumption
How can we live joyfully amongst all this
tension?

So much stress over success
Now we're all depressed

What happened to home?
We ruined it.

Art

Sparkling eyes extinguished
They wear a mask

Time took their smile
Void took their heart

Numbness became default
Because loneliness kills

Rejection took pieces of their soul
Pain took their flesh, drew blood

Everlasting, Art is their escape